Biko Learns Ancient Traditions

Goddess Nini

DEDICATION

Honor and Reverence to the Ancestors, my Mother Anne Suvenise Jules, my father Joseph E. Jules Louissaint.
My Grandmother and Grandfather, Great Grandmothers and Great Grandfathers six generations before. I honor the Spirits of Earth, Water, Fire and Air.
For I Am My Ancestors and I vow to embrace, love, and teach our children to honor and revere Ancestral Traditions.

INITIATION

Although different cultures pay honor and reverence to those who have departed, Christianity always condemn those who choose to do the same, especially in Afro-American Spirituality such as Vodou. The condemnation is based on biblical scriptures that elude the dead being unaware of any honor conferred on them and to let the dead bury the dead. If we should not acknowledge the dead, why are schools, airports, hospitals, and streets named after famous people who have died? Why are monuments erected and holidays established to commemorate heroic personages?

We must embrace our vibrant culture and way of life. The ancient ways of our ancestors, the ancient ways of living. Honoring those who were here before us. Those who paved the way for our liberty, who nurtured, cherished, and gave up their lives for freedom and justice. Those who left wisdom and knowledge for us to live more abundant lives in balance and harmony with nature, everyone, and everything around us.

In Ancient Traditions, Grandmothers and Grandfathers spent a lot of time teaching their children, grandchildren, and children in the villages the ancient ways. They were called elders.
Elders made sure the community was always in order. They also enjoyed teaching the younger children because children are closer to the realm of the Ancestors and the Elders are closer to returning to the Spirit realm. In "Biko Learns Ancient Traditions" Grandmother Alouma teaches her grandson Biko traditions of the ancients. Rise up, Goddesses and Gods, Queens and Kings. Let us call on our powerful Ancestors, honor them, and teach our children their ways so we take back all that we have lost.

School was in recess and Biko sat under the oak tree, running his fingers through the dirt. He suddenly looked up and noticed the clear blue sky with pure white clouds drifting by slowly. The cool breeze of the wind gently stroked his face; the tree branches swayed in harmony to the movement of the wind. Biko closed his eyes and leaned his head on the tree trunk.

"Biko," "Biko," the voice calls again. Biko, a little startled, looks up; it was Grandmother Alouma. He jumps up and hugs his grandmother and Grandma Alouma kisses him on the forehead. Holding her folding chair, Biko reaches to take the chair from his grandmother.

"Oh, my child," said Grandmother Alouma, "Please allow me, I'm still vibrant my dear," She pulls the chair from the bag, unfolds it, and sat next to Biko.

Biko turns towards his grandmother, "I miss Grandpa Ati," says Biko; Grandmother Alouma looks at Biko and smiles. "I'm sure you do. I miss him being here as well.

But remember, your grandfather is always with us, says Grandmother Alouma. "But he's not here grandmother", replied Biko. "We must not forget that when a person dies, they become special angels," said Grandmother.

"Really? asked Biko, as his eyes widen. "Yes indeed. Your grandfather was a wise man. He loved everyone and was loyal, honest, and brave. He respected everyone, stood for what was right, and wanted everyone to live in harmony. He offered help to anyone in need. If he could not help, he would find someone else to help the person in need.

He would pay for people's groceries and helped people find solutions to their problems. Grandfather Ati loved children. Children were a weakness for him. I think he had extra energy because he never complained of being tired, never," said Grandmother. "He was a super-hero Grandma," said Biko. Grandmother Alouma smiled and said, "Well, that's a good way to describe him."

"Biko, your grandfather is now an Ancestor, a special angel. You can speak to your Ancestors," said Grandmother. Biko raises his eyebrows, "How do I speak to Grandpa Ati, asked Biko? Grandma Alouma looked up towards the clear blue sky and smiled, "You can speak to your Grandfather anytime, just as you are speaking to me, my child."

"Will Grandpa respond, asked Biko? Grandmother Alouma laughed, "yes my dear, but not in the way I respond."

Biko starred at his grandmother with a slight grin on his face, got up, and went inside the house. He returned with two glasses filled with cold water.

He handed one of the glasses to Grandmother Alouma and leaned on the tree trunk. There was complete silence as they drank water and gazed into the clear blue sky.

That night Biko sat up in his bed, looking through the window. He could see the deep blue sky filled with stars. He began to speak. "Hello, Grandpa Ati.

Grandma told me to speak to you anytime. So please hear me. I miss you and all the fun we used to have together. You promised to teach me to connect with Mother Earth, but you went away. Biko sighed, I love you, Grandpa. Goodnight." Biko tucked himself under the cover and fell asleep.

Biko slowly opened his eyes. The rays of the sunlight pierced through the window and filled the room with a warm sensation. The trees appeared to be wearing golden crowns.

He could hear the birds chirping. A fruity and familiar smell tickled his nose. He knew it was the smell of grandmother's favorite breakfast tea. "I smell the chamomile, peppermint, and lemongrass," Biko said to himself. Making tea was a sunrise tradition for Grandmother Alouma.

Biko rushed to the bathroom, brushed his teeth, washed his face, and changed his clothes. He looked for his favorite white T-shirt with the picture of the djembe drum on it. He quietly tiptoed downstairs and slowly walked towards his grandmother, who was busy being creative in the kitchen.

"Good day, Biko. How was your night?" asked Grandmother Alouma. "How did you know it was me, Grandma," asked Biko as he turned and noticed his Cousin Zaka sipping tea. Biko rushed and hugged Zaka. He rarely sees cousin Zaka because he is busy working on a project that seems to be a secret. "How is your Mother Biko?" asked Zaka?

Just as Biko was about to respond, the phone rang. He rushed to answer, "Hello!" "Hi, Mom. No, not yet." "Grandma, my mom wants to speak to you."

Grandmother Alouma responds, "Let her know that I will have to call her back if she's ok." "Grandma will call you back, mom. See you tomorrow. I love you," says Biko and hangs up the phone.

Biko walks back towards the kitchen table and sits down. Grandma places his favorite mug in front of him full of tea. "I love the smell and the taste of this tea, thank you, Grandma," said Biko. Grandmother replies, "The herbs in the tea are gifts from Mother Nature.

These herbs are medicine that is necessary to keep us healthy and strong. They have been used for thousands of years to heal disease in the body and bring the body to its natural balance. We must always remember the ancient traditions of the Ancestors and live by them."

Grandma Alouma turns around, walks towards the kitchen door, and steps outside. She stands there for a few minutes, pours three drops of coffee in the ground, takes a sip, and walks back inside the kitchen. "Why do you always pour coffee outside, Grandmother asked Biko? "It is called a libation.

We pour a libation for the Ancestors and spirits of nature to honor them, thank them, and call on them to assist us in life. For the Ancestors live through us. We must always honor their wisdom by teaching our children and grandchildren the ancient ways. This is how culture is preserved and respected," said Grandmother Alouma as she placed breakfast on the table.

Biko was so excited as he said, "tell me more, Grandmother. I want to learn more about the Ancient Traditions and the Ancestors. "I'll tell you more another day, my child.

We must have breakfast so we can leave for our adventure to the marketplace," replied Grandmother Alouma. "I love you, Grandma," said Biko. "I love you more, my child," responded Grandmother Alouma.

ABOUT THE AUTHOR

Goddess Nini is a Healer, Spiritualist, and Writer. Born Annide Jules, in Nassau Bahamas, she always found herself attracted to "stranger things" growing up. Considered the black sheep of her family she found the courage to take the "road less traveled," dismissed "Christianity" in doctrination and journeyed into Spirituality and Ancestor Veneration. Through daily journaling and meditation which were outlets on her lonely spiritual journey, she became passionate about writing.

Annide has worked over 20 years with children, teens, and women as a social worker. She has identified two key ingredients to begin the healing process. These two ingredients are reconnecting with nature and ancestor veneration. Therefore, she dedicates her life to help people, especially children heal. Goddess Nini is ecstatic to debut her book "Biko Learns Ancient Traditions," the first of a 3 element children's books. She invites all children and anyone who wish, to take the journey with Biko, as he learns about ancient traditions.